Private View

A Play

Václav Havel

A Samuel French Acting Edition

SAMUELFRENCH-LONDON.CO.UK
SAMUELFRENCH.COM

PRIVATE VIEW

Produced by BBC TV for the 1978/79 Play for Today season with the following cast:

Ferdinand Vaněk	Michael Crawford
Michael	Ian Richardson
Vera	Zena Walker

Producer Innes Lloyd
Director Claude Watham

The action takes place in Michael's and Vera's living-room

Time—the present

CHARACTERS

Ferdinand Vaněk
Michael
Vera

Also by Václav Havel published by Samuel French Ltd

Audience

PRIVATE VIEW

The living-room of Michael's and Vera's flat

The flat is freshly decorated and over-stuffed with antiques, including a Turkish yataghan, a Baroque confessional, a Gothic Madonna and a musical Rococo clock on the mantelpiece. Other furniture includes a sideboard, a coffee table and a hi-fi set

Michael and Vera are on stage

The latest US pop hit record starts to blare out. Over the music there is the sound of the doorbell in the front hall

Vera turns off the record and the music stops abruptly

Vera The doorbell.
Michael Oh? Didn't hear it.
Vera Must be Ferdinand. He's late.
Michael I'll go.

    Michael exits

Short pause. The front door is opened, off

Ferdinand (*off*) Hello, Michael!
Michael (*off. Loud, cordial*) Hello, Ferdinand! Come in, come in!

The front door is closed

    We were beginning to get worried. We were afraid perhaps you weren't coming tonight!

Michael and Ferdinand enter, Ferdinand carrying a bunch of roses

Ferdinand Sorry to be late. Hello, Vera!
Vera Hello, dear. How are you? Long time no see!
Michael We were afraid perhaps you weren't able to make it.
Vera We've been longing to see you!
Michael It's been a long time!
Ferdinand Yes, hasn't it?
Vera We've missed you, you know!

Michael Now, what will you have? What do you say about some bourbon eh?

Ferdinand All right with me.

Michael exits

Vera Michael brought back a special bourbon from the States, you see.

Ferdinand Oh? (*He fumbles with the wrapped-up bunch of roses he has brought*) Here—(*he proffers them to Vera*) a small offering.

Vera For me? How lovely! Oh, but they are beautiful! Darling, look what I've got! Look at all those beautiful roses! How very kind of you Ferdinand! You never forget, do you. (*Smelling them*) Mmnn—they do smell nice! Thank you, dear. (*Walking off to put them in a vase*) I must find a pretty vase for them, mustn't I?

Ferdinand I'm glad you like them.

Vera exits

Pause. Ferdinand looks around, absorbed in and astonished at what he sees

Michael (*off*) Ice?

Ferdinand Well, yes—

Michael (*off*) Soda?

Ferdinand Well—I—

Michael (*off*) On the rocks, then?

Ferdinand Whatever you say. (*Short pause*) Listen, where am I? What's happened to your flat? It's all been changed!

Vera returns with the vase

Vera But of course, dear. All Michael's work! He's worked on it ever so hard! Well, you know how he is. Once he gets started on something, he never lets go until everything's exactly the way he planned it.

Michael enters with the drinks

Michael As a matter of fact, I only finished the whole thing the day before yesterday. Nobody's seen it yet. So this is an occasion, old boy! We're having a little Private View in here tonight! (*He puts down the tray of drinks on the coffee table*) And here are the drinks.

Ferdinand (*still looking around in amazement*) Where on earth did you find all this stuff? Good heavens! Look at all those things! Where did you find them?

Michael Wasn't easy, you know. Well, I did have an "in" here and there, a few antique dealers, some art collectors, that sort of thing. But of course I had to make many new contacts as well. Thing is, one must never give up. Not even when one doesn't find straight away precisely what one is looking for.

Vera Fabulous the way it's coming out, isn't it?

Ferdinand Mmnn—

Vera To be quite honest, I didn't really expect it to come out so well. The point is, if you want to give your place a real face, it's no good just being fond of antiques. You've got to know where to find them. And to have that extra sense of presenting them the best way in your house. To know how to mix them with modern furniture, for example, and so on. Well, as it turned out, Michael managed all right, didn't he? Fabulous, isn't it? Not a dud. Not a slip-up!

Michael (*distributing the drinks*) Well, here's your drink, old boy. Darling? Welcome to our "new" home!

Vera We've missed you, Ferdinand, you know.

Michael I kept wondering—I mean, while I was working on this place—what's he going to say when it's all done up, and he walks in, looks around, and sees all these things!

Ferdinand Well, cheers!

They all clink glasses

Vera Cheers!
Michael Cheers!

They all drink. Short pause

Of course, if Vera hadn't supported me, I'm sure it would have never come out as well as this. Besides, it wasn't just a matter of support and understanding, she actually helped, you know. For example, over the fireplace—you see the Turkish yataghan? Well? What do you say about it?

Ferdinand Very nice—

Michael How does it fit in with the rest?

Ferdinand Very well.

Michael There you are, you see! Vera found it all by herself! She even hung it over there! And all the time she had no idea I'd been looking for something exactly like this to hang over the fireplace. Well, what do you say? Amazing, isn't it?

Ferdinand Yes, it is—

Vera (*after a short pause*) Good gracious, what are we standing around for? Why don't we sit down?

Michael and Vera sit down

Ferdinand? Come on, do sit down!

Ferdinand sits down, staring in astonishment at a Baroque confessional

Ferdinand Thanks. That vast thing over there—

Vera Fabulous, isn't it?

Ferdinand Looks like a confessional—

Michael It is a confessional!

Ferdinand Good Lord! Where did you get it?

Michael Just think. Was a real stroke of luck, you know. Well, I happened to hear there was an old disused church to be scrapped, so naturally I took off at once and drove straight down there. And—here you see the result! Managed to get it from the sacristan for only three hundred crowns!

Ferdinand Is that all?

Michael Not bad, eh? Genuine Baroque! Take a look!

Ferdinand What are you going to do with it?

Michael What do you mean, what are we going to do with it! Don't you like it?

Ferdinand It's all right—

Michael But it's a marvellous object, isn't it? We love it, don't we, darling?

Vera Just look at it! Fabulous workmanship! Michael really got a bargain there, don't you think? (*Short pause*) What do you say about the dining room?

Ferdinand Where?

Vera (*pointing*) Behind you dear! You must turn around! See? Up those two steps. Back there.

Ferdinand (*turns round*) Mmnn—Cosy, isn't it?

Vera Good idea, what? Just plain, simple country style!

Ferdinand Mmnn—

Michael (*after a short pause*) You know what gives me the greatest pleasure of all?

Ferdinand What?

Michael This Gothic Madonna! Trouble was, I had to find one that would fit exactly into this niche, and as luck would have it, of course, I kept finding Madonnas that were either too tall, or too short—

Ferdinand You couldn't have adjusted the niche?

Michael That was precisely what I didn't want to do. I think only in this way the whole ensemble has the right dimensions.

Vera That's the way he is. Instead of adjusting a niche, he'll wear out his feet running about!

Pause

Michael Well, how about you, then? When are you two going to have a go at it?

Ferdinand At what?

Michael Your flat, of course.

Ferdinand I don't know—

Michael About time you did something with it, old boy. You don't want to go on living in that messy half-way house for ever!

Ferdinand I don't seem to notice it any more—

Michael If you don't feel up to it, well, why doesn't Eva have a go? After all, she's got plenty of time.

Vera I believe doing something like this would actually be very good for her. Put her back on her feet.

Michael We'll do our best to help her, if she doesn't know how to go about it.

Vera Michael is a bit of an expert now, you know. He'll be happy to advise her, show her what to do, where to begin, what things to look for—

Michael Good gracious! I'll be glad to let her know what's available and where, who are the dealers she ought to see—

Vera Exactly! It's a good idea! Listen, Ferdinand, why don't you just hand it over to Eva!

Ferdinand I'm afraid, Eva isn't very good at this sort of thing—

Vera We know that, dear, but perhaps you might be able to awaken a bit of interest in her.

Michael You've got to do something about that flat of yours, damn it!

Vera You see, Michael and I believe that a man's life is determined by his immediate surroundings. If you have what we call a place with a face, then, whether you like it or not, your life, too, suddenly begins to acquire a definite face, sort of new dimension, new rhythm, new content, new order—am I right, darling?

Michael She's right, old boy! You see, same way a man should care about what he eats, he ought to mind what he happens to eat it with, and what he eats if off, what he wipes himself with, what he puts on, what he washes himself in, what he sleeps in, and so on. The point is, once you start one thing, you soon find you must start another, and that will lead you to something else again, and so a sort of concatenation of things begins to form. And when you go on this way, *it just means you're somehow raising your life on to a higher cultural level, you're acquiring a deeper inner harmony*, and all this is bound in the end to affect your relationship with others. Am I right, darling?

Vera He's right, Ferdinand. If you two began to mind a bit about the way you live, I'm sure you'd get on much better!

Ferdinand But we get on all right—

Vera Oh, come off it, dear!

Ferdinand Really, we do—

Vera I realize you'd rather not talk about it. But you see, Michael and I have been discussing you two a lot lately, we've been thinking about you a great deal—and frankly, we're a bit worried about the way you live!

Michael It's kindly meant, old boy. It's in your own interests.

Vera Remember, you're our best friend. We're both very fond of you. We do hope, somehow or other, it all gets sorted out for you at last.

Ferdinand But what's there to be sorted out?

Vera (*after a short pause*) Oh, never mind. Shall I light the fire?

Ferdinand Not on my account—

Michael How about some music, then?

Vera Michael brought back a lot of new records from the States, you see. As a matter of fact, we were listening to one of the latest pop hits just as you rang. Would you like to hear it?

Ferdinand A bit later, perhaps?

Pause. Suddenly, off, but loudly, the clock on the mantelpiece begins to play a period tune

(*Starting*) What's that?

Vera It's our new clock.

Michael On the mantelpiece.
Ferdinand Oh—
Michael Genuine Rococo!
Vera Lovely, isn't it?
Ferdinand Mmnn—

The clock stops playing. Pause. This whole sequence will be repeated twice more later on

Vera Well, tell us about yourself. How're things with you?
Ferdinand Much the same.
Vera Is it true you're now working in a brewery?
Ferdinand Yes—
Vera How awful! (*Pause. She points to the tray on the sideboard*) Darling, would you mind passing the tray.
Michael Sorry. Yes, of course—

He brings the tray and puts it down on the coffee table

Here we are.
Vera Help yourself.
Ferdinand What is it?
Michael Vera's speciality! Groombles gratinés.
Ferdinand Groombles? Never heard of them.
Vera We've come to like them very much, lately. Michael brought back a big box of them from the States. Shells and all.
Michael Mind you, Vera really knows how to make them!
Vera The whole point is, one must watch for the precise moment they begin to puff up, and take them out of the oven just before they begin to go down.
Michael Why don't you try one? Go on!
Ferdinand How do you eat them?
Vera Just take the shell and scoop them out. Here's a spoon.
Ferdinand (*taking the spoon*) Thanks.

Ferdinand takes one of the shells and scoops out its contents with a spoon. He eats with great concentration. Michael and Vera watch him tensely

Michael Well? What do you say?
Ferdinand (*smacking his lips*) Good—
Michael Aren't they?
Ferdinand You mean you've made them on my account?

Vera Well, after all, this is an occasion, we're having our Private View tonight, aren't we?

Ferdinand Reminds me of blackberries a bit.

Vera Could be, because I put a few drops of woodpeak on them just to add that little extra something.

Ferdinand Of what?

Michael Woodpeak.

Vera I hit on it all by myself!

Ferdinand Did you?

Michael Good idea, isn't it? Mind you, Vera has a real talent for cooking. Not a week goes by without her making a new discovery, and each time it's her own fantasy at work! Take last Saturday, for instance—what was it we had? Oh yes, liver with chestnuts. Simply delicious, you know. Well, I mean, would it ever occur to you to put woodpeak on groombles?

Ferdinand No—

Michael There you are!

Ferdinand puts away the empty shell and wipes his mouth with a napkin

Vera Mind you, it's a pleasure to cook for Michael. He can appreciate and praise even the most humble idea I happen to have. And when I manage to concoct something really good, it gives him so much pleasure. If he just mechanically gobbled up everything that's on his plate without realizing what he's eating, I don't really think I'd bother.

Ferdinand I see what you mean—

Michael But in fact, there are other aspects to it, as well. When you know there's an interesting dinner, a new gastronomic surprise, so to speak, waiting for you at home, then of course you're looking forward to going back. You're far less likely to hang about the bars with your pals. Perhaps you might think it's a minor matter, but I believe that even these little things actually make up the cement which keeps a family together and helps to create the good feeling that you've got a real base right at home. Don't you agree?

Ferdinand Yes, certainly—

Vera (*after a pause*) Well, and how's Eva? Has she now learned a little about cooking?

Ferdinand But she's always done the cooking—

Vera All right, but *how*!

Ferdinand Well, I can't say I don't like it—

Vera You've got used to it, that's all. I'm sorry, dear, but for instance that roast we had in your house before Christmas—it was before Christmas, wasn't it?

Ferdinand Yes—

Vera I'm sorry, but it was terrible. You remember, darling?

Michael Good heavens, yes!

Ferdinand I'm afraid Eva was a bit nervous that night.

Vera I'm sorry, but this sort of thing should simply never happen to a cook. What does she feed you, actually?

Ferdinand We seem to have cold dinners—mostly—

Vera Saturdays, too?

Ferdinand Well, sometimes, there's a hot meal—a steak, for example—

Michael Listen, old boy, I know it's none of my business, but supposing you send Eva to one of those classes? After all, she's got plenty of time.

Vera Eva? You must be joking! You mean you can visualize Eva in any sort of class?

Michael Well, no, now that you mention it.

Vera If she'd only learn to cook, she'd be much more self-assured! Straight away! But will she listen to reason? Not on your life! She's always somewhere, heaven knows where, up in the clouds—

Ferdinand But I don't mind her cooking—I think it's all right—

Michael Oh, come on, old boy!

Ferdinand Really, I do—

Michael I realize you'd rather not talk about it. But you see, Vera and I have been discussing you two a lot lately, we've been thinking about you a great deal—and, frankly, we're a bit worried about the way you live.

Vera It's kindly meant, dear. It's in your own interests.

Michael Remember, you're our best friend. We're both very fond of you. We do hope, somehow or other, it all gets sorted out for you at last.

Ferdinand But what's there to be sorted out?

Michael (*after a short pause*) Oh, never mind. Shall I light the fire?

Ferdinand Not on my account.

Vera How about some music then? Michael brought back a lot of new records from the States, you see.

Ferdinand A bit later, perhaps?

Pause. Suddenly, off, but loudly, the clock on the mantelpiece begins to play a period tune

(*Starting*) What's that?

Vera It's our new clock.

Michael On the mantelpiece.

Ferdinand Oh—

Michael Genuine Rococo!

Vera Lovely, isn't it?

Ferdinand Mmnn—

The clock stops playing

Michael (*after a pause*) What do you actually do in there? That brewery.

Ferdinand I handle casks.

Michael What's that supposed to mean?

Ferdinand Well, I roll the barrels, you know—

Michael Good God! Pretty rough on you, isn't it?

Ferdinand It's not too bad.

Michael (*after a pause*) Darling, shouldn't we take Ferdinand to look in on little Pete?

Vera In a moment, dear, he might still wake up now.

Ferdinand How is Pete?

Michael Oh, he's incredible! I was away in the States only a fortnight, you know, and when I came back, believe it or not, I could hardly recognize him! That's the sort of leap forward he made in that short time.

Vera He's so curious about everything—

Michael Very bright—

Vera Very sensitive—

Michael Excellent memory—

Vera And you know, he's such a pretty little boy!

Michael Just as an example. Imagine the sort of thing he asked me this morning. I don't think I've told you yet, darling. Well, all of a sudden he comes up to me and asks, Daddy, can a frog drown? What do you think of that! Fantastic, isn't he?

Vera Did he really ask that? He asked if a frog could drown?

Michael Just think! He comes up to me and asks, Daddy, can a frog drown?

Vera Fabulous! Thing like that would never even cross one's mind. Can a frog drown! Fabulous! Fabulous!

Michael Listen, old boy. I often say to myself, this is the only thing in life that makes sense, having a child and being able to bring it up! It's an amazing confrontation with the mystery of life, you know, sort of school in which you learn to respect life. Those who didn't have this experience can never understand what it means.

Vera He's right, Ferdinand! Really, it's a very strange and a very beautiful experience! One fine day a tiny creature appears here, and you know that he's yours, that he wouldn't be here if it weren't for you, you made him, he's here now, he lives his own life, and he keeps growing up right in front of your eyes, and then he begins to walk, and to prattle, to think and to ask questions—well, you must agree, it's a miracle!

Ferdinand Yes, it is.

Michael You see, having a child changes a man a lot. All of a sudden one begins to see things in a new and different light, one gets a deeper insight into life, into nature, and people. Whether you like it or not, your life suddenly begins to acquire a sort of new dimension, new rhythm, new content, new order—isn't it so, darling?

Vera Absolutely! Well, take the responsibility you must assume, all at once. It's up to you what sort of man he's going to be, what he's going to feel, to think, to experience—

Michael And not only that. Just because it was you who brought him into this world, who offered it to him for his use, and who's trying to give him some bearings in it, you find that you, too, begin to feel infinitely more responsible for the world which surrounds this little boy. You know what I mean?

Ferdinand Mmnn—

Michael I wouldn't have believed it, but now I see how a child can give one an entirely new perspective, an entirely new scale of values. And one begins to understand that the most important thing is what one's going to do for the child, what sort of home, what sort of start in life one's going to give him. And in the light of this enormous responsibility most of the things one used to consider of world-shaking importance turn out to be nothing but trifles.

Vera What was it he asked? Can a frog drown? Well, there you see what a little head like that can come up with!

Ferdinand Mmnn—

Michael (*after a pause*) Well, what about you two, then?

Ferdinand What about us?

Michael Why don't you have a child?

Ferdinand I don't know—

Vera I suppose Eva doesn't want one, does she?

Ferdinand Oh, no—she does—

Vera I don't understand that girl! Is she so afraid of all the trouble that comes with it? I mean, if she really wanted to have a baby, good heavens, you'd have had it long ago!

Michael You're only harming yourselves when you don't try and do something about it! I mean, specially for you and Eva, a child would be the best solution! It'd help you to see many things more wisely, more realistically, more reasonably—

Vera And I'm sure it'd put your relationship back on its feet by providing your lives with a common purpose.

Michael It'd do Eva a world of good!

Vera You'd see how she'd change!

Michael It'd wake up the woman in her again!

Vera Teach her how to take care of the house!

Michael Keep it clean—

Vera And tidy—

Michael Take better care of you—

Vera And of herself—

Michael Honestly, Ferdinand, please believe us, you ought to have a child!

Vera You can't imagine how much we wish for you to have one!

Michael Really, old boy, we do, you know!

Ferdinand I believe you—

Vera (*after a pause*) Mind you, I've seen women who aren't at all affected by having a child. In which case I'm sorry for the children!

Michael Mind you, one can't expect a child to be a sort of cure-all for all your ills, to solve all your problems. That sort of approach wouldn't be right, either. After all, there must exist some basic prerequisites.

Vera Absolutely! Take Michael, for instance, he really is an ideal husband! He works so hard in the office, you know, often I can't help feeling really sorry for him! All because he wants to bring home some money! And in spite of all his work he spends most of his free time with his family and on his house! Well, take his doing up this flat. I mean, he'd come back from the office, and instead of having a little rest, he'd start to beaver away all over again. Just because he wants the boy to grow up in nice surroundings from the very beginning, and to learn respect and love for nice things! And on top of that he even manages to find time for our little boy!

Michael Well, of course, Vera is simply marvellous! Just try and think what it means to do all the shopping, look after the little boy, cook, do all the cleaning, all the washing, and on top of that for weeks having to cope with the whole place in a shambles! And yet, in spite of it she manages to look the way she does! That's something, you know. I must say, I admire her more and more every day.

Vera Much of this simply boils down to the fact that our marriage works.

Michael It surely does! We understand each other completely. I don't recall there's been any serious quarrel, lately.

Vera We happen to be interested in one another. Same time, we don't restrict one another too much, we don't shackle one another!

Michael We're far too kind and attentive towards each other to do anything like that! Same time, we try not to bother one another too much with our attentions.

Vera And there're always things for us to talk about, because we happen to be lucky in having the same sense of humour!

Michael Same ideas about happiness—

Vera Same interests—

Michael Same tastes—

Vera Same views on family life—

Michael And what's really important, we understand each other perfectly in bed.

Vera Oh, absolutely! That's extremely important! Well, you see, Michael is quite marvellous! He's wild and gentle, healthily egoistic and overwhelmingly sensitive and self-sacrificing, passionate, spontaneous and subtly refined!

Michael Which is all Vera's doing in the first place, of course, because she manages to go on exciting and attracting me!

Vera You'd be surprised, Ferdinand, how often we do it! And the only reason it is this way, you know, is because we always come to it as if it was the first time! So that every time it is for us somehow new, different, unique, unforgettable! The point is, each time we get completely absorbed in it, so it can never become a matter of habit for us, or some dull routine.

Michael The point is, to be a good wife doesn't mean to Vera merely being a good housewife or a good mother. She feels correctly that *it's above all a matter of being a good mistress!* That's also why she's taking such good care of herself, so that with all the hard work she's got to do, she manages to keep looking really sexy! In fact, she's most ravishing just when she's *working the hardest!*

Vera Remember, darling, day before yesterday—I was scrubbing the floor, and you arrived unexpectedly?

Michael Beautiful, wasn't it?

Vera Why do you think Michael isn't attracted to other girls? Because he realizes he's got a real woman at home who knows how to give and take—and not some sloppy little plain Jane with a pail and a mop!

Michael The point is, Vera has remained as smashing as ever. In fact, I'd almost say, after she had Pete she sort of ripened. The body she's got now! It's a knock-out! So fresh and young! Well, you can judge for yourself. Darling, do you mind just opening your dress a little bit? May I? (*Short pause while he lowers Vera's dress at the top, revealing her bosom*) Well, what did I tell you! Look at her bosom! Exquisite, isn't it?

Ferdinand First class—

Michael For example, you know what I like to do?

Ferdinand No—what?

Michael Well, I kiss her ear and her neck in turn—she loves it! I like it too, as a matter of fact. This is how I do it. See?

He begins to kiss her as described

Vera (*starting to sigh in mounting excitement*) No! Stop it! Darling, please, stop! No! Can't you wait? Later, all right? Darling, please!

Michael stops kissing her

Michael After we've finished our little chat, we're going to show you some more, so you'll see what sophisticated things we do to one another.

Ferdinand Won't my being around make you nervous?

Vera Oh, come on, dear! Don't be silly! Remember, you're our best friend!

Michael We'll be only too happy to demonstrate to you the things that can be done in this respect.

Vera Shall I cover my bosom now, darling?

Michael Yes, for the moment.

A pause while Vera adjusts her dress

Vera How about you two, then? How do you manage?

Ferdinand What do you mean?

Vera You sleep together at all?

Ferdinand Well, yes—now and then—

Vera Not very often though, I bet!

Ferdinand It depends—

Vera How is it, then?

Ferdinand How should it be? Seems normal—

Michael I bet you do it haphazardly, carelessly, so it's soon over and done with?

Ferdinand We do it the best way we know—

Vera I simply don't understand that girl! She doesn't seem to be trying at all, not even in this respect.

Michael Can't you make her a bit more committed to it?

Ferdinand Well, we aren't so very concerned about it, actually—

Vera There you are! That's precisely where you're making your most serious mistake! Good heavens, it's so important, and you just ignore it! That's why things are the way they are between you two! And all the time, what's needed is so very little! Who knows, it might even put your relationship back on its feet!

Michael After all, it'd be good for Eva, you'd see how she'd change.

Vera It'd wake up the woman in her again!

Michael Teach her how to take better care of the house—

Vera Of you—

Michael Of herself—

Vera And the difference it'd make to you! Just think, you'd suddenly lose all interest in hanging about the bars with those pals of yours—

Michael Chasing after the barmaids—
Vera Boozing—
Ferdinand But I don't chase after any barmaids—
Vera Oh, come off it, dear!
Ferdinand Really, I don't—
Vera I realize you'd rather not talk about it. But you see, Michael and I have been discussing you two a lot lately, we've been thinking about you a great deal—and frankly we're a bit worried about the way you live.
Michael It's kindly meant, old boy. It's in your own interests.
Vera Remember, you're our best friend. We're both very fond of you. We do hope, somehow or other, it all gets sorted out for you at last!
Ferdinand But what's there to be sorted out?
Vera (*after a short pause*) Oh, never mind. Shall I light the fire?
Ferdinand Not on my account—
Michael How about some music, then?
Vera Michael brought back a lot of new records from the States, you see.
Ferdinand A bit later, perhaps?

Pause. Suddenly, off, but loudly, the clock on the mantelpiece begins to play a period tune

(*Starting*) What's that?
Vera It's our new clock.
Michael On the mantelpiece.
Ferdinand Oh—
Michael Genuine Rococo!
Vera Lovely, isn't it?
Ferdinand Mmnn—

The clock stops playing

Michael (*after a pause*) Well, whatever you say, it's an amazing object!
Ferdinand The clock?
Michael The Madonna.
Ferdinand Ah!
Michael You notice the dramatic tension between her and the yataghan?
Ferdinand Mmnn—

Vera (*after a pause*) I bet you've never used any woodpeak!
Ferdinand Not really—
Vera Michael could bring you some next time he goes to the States, if you like.
Ferdinand Could he?
Michael Sure, no trouble.
Vera (*after a pause*) How about another groomble?
Ferdinand No more, thank you—
Michael (*after a pause*) Why didn't you bring Eva along, actually?
Ferdinand She wasn't feeling very well—
Michael I know it's none of my business, but you ought to take her out now and then to see people. Least she'd have an excuse to dress up from time to time, put on some make-up, wash her hair—
Ferdinand But she does wash her hair—
Michael Oh, come on, old boy!
Ferdinand Really, she does—
Michael I realize you'd rather not talk about it. But it's kindly meant, you know!
Vera We're both very fond of you.
Michael Remember, you're our best friend.
Ferdinand I remember—

Pause. The clock plays its tune again. This time, as in all further instances, without comment

Michael Did you get my card from the States?
Ferdinand Oh, it was from you, was it?
Michael You mean, you didn't know?
Ferdinand Should have occurred to me—
Vera (*after a pause*) What was it Pete asked you, darling? Can a frog drown?
Michael That's what he asked. Just think!
Vera Fabulous! Fabulous!
Michael (*after a pause*) Come on! Do help yourself!
Ferdinand No more for me, thank you—
Vera (*after a pause*) You know what we started doing again?
Ferdinand No. What?
Vera Going to the sauna!
Ferdinand Did you?

Vera We go once a week, and you'd be surprised how good we feel now. Does wonders for one's nervous system, you know.

Michael How about coming along with us?

Ferdinand Well, I don't really—

Vera Come on! Why don't you?

Ferdinand I don't really think I can find the time—

Michael Sorry, old boy, but you're making a big mistake. It'd give you a bit of a lift, you'd be better off mentally and physically. It'd do a world of good to your nervous system. It'd be far better for you, and it'd take far less of your time, than all this hanging about the bars with those questionable pals of yours!

Ferdinand Who's that? Whom do you mean, exactly?

Michael Well, all those has-beens, you know, those failures— Landovsky, for instance—

Ferdinand I don't think they're has-beens, or failures!

Vera Oh come off it, dear!

Ferdinand Really, I don't.

Vera I realize you'd rather not talk about it. But it's kindly meant!

Michael We're very fond of you.

Vera You're our best friend.

Ferdinand I know—

Pause. The clock plays its tune again

Michael Let me tell you what Vera promised me!

Ferdinand What's that?

Michael That next year she's going to give me another child!

Ferdinand Good for you—

Vera I believe Michael deserves it. Really! (*Pause*) Let me tell you what he brought me back from the States!

Ferdinand What's that?

Vera An electric almond-peeler!

Michael We must show it to you, it's a marvellous object!

Vera And how useful!

Michael You see, Vera happens to use almonds a great deal in her cooking, so it saves her a lot of time and labour.

Ferdinand I see what you mean—

Vera (*after a pause*) Go on, dear, help yourself!

Ferdinand No more for me, thanks—

Michael (*after a pause*) Listen, Ferdinand—

Ferdinand Mmnn—

Michael You do any writing at all these days?
Ferdinand Not much—
Michael That's what we thought.
Ferdinand I had to take this job, so I haven't much time for it now, and it's hard to concentrate—
Michael But as far as I recall, you didn't do all that much writing even before you took this job.
Ferdinand Not all that much, no—
Vera Listen, when you took this job, wasn't there somewhere in the back of your mind—I mean, didn't you think that perhaps it might be a good excuse for you not to go on with your writing?
Ferdinand Good God, no!
Michael Well then, why do you actually write so little? Is it because you just can't any longer? Or is it some sort of momentary crisis?
Ferdinand Hard to say—present times, I suppose—things that go on. One has a feeling of futility—
Michael Sorry, old boy, but it's my impression that the "present times" are just an excuse for you, much as that job at the brewery, and that the real reason is deep down in yourself! You seem to have simply fallen apart, given up, opted out! It's become too much trouble for you now to strive for anything, to struggle, to grapple with difficulties.
Vera He's right, Ferdinand! About time you pulled yourself together again! Why don't you try and get organized—
Michael Straighten out your problems with Eva—
Vera Start a family—
Michael Give a face to your place—
Vera Stop wasting your time—
Michael Stop boozing—
Vera Start going to the sauna—
Michael In short, begin to lead a sort of decent, healthy, reasonable life!
Ferdinand But I don't think I'm doing anything unreasonable—
Michael Oh, come on, old boy!
Ferdinand Really, I don't—
Michael I realize you'd rather not talk about it. But it's kindly meant!
Vera We're very fond of you.
Michael You're our best friend.

Vera We do hope, somehow or other, it all gets sorted out for you
  at last!
Michael Shall I light the fire?
Ferdinand Not on my account—
Vera How about some music, then? Michael brought back a lot of
  new records from the States, you see.
Ferdinand A bit later, perhaps?

Pause. The clock plays its tune again

Michael Listen, Ferdinand—
Ferdinand Mmnn—
Michael But you're going to level with us, OK? Listen, are you
  being quite serious about that brewery?
Ferdinand What do you mean?
Michael Look here, old boy, I hope you don't mind, but we
  simply can't see the point!
Vera Good heavens! To waste your life in this way, bury yourself
  in some stinking brewery, damage your health doing that sort of
  work—
Michael Gestures like that are absolutely pointless! What are you
  trying to prove? You think anybody's impressed? Nobody gives
  a damn about that sort of thing any more!
Ferdinand I'm sorry, but the situation I was in, well, it was the
  only thing I could find—
Michael Oh, come on, old boy! Don't tell me you couldn't have
  found something more appropriate! I mean, provided you really
  wanted to and tried a bit harder! I'm sure with a little more
  effort and a bit less romanticism you could've been long since
  working on the editorial staff of some newspaper or publishing
  house.
Vera Look, you're basically an intelligent, hard-working fellow,
  also you've talent, that was made clear by your former writing—
  then why are you all of a sudden so afraid to meet the challenges
  of life?
Michael Life is hard and the world is divided. Our country has
  been written off by everybody, nobody's going to help us, our
  lot is pretty bad now and it's going to get worse, and you won't
  change it, you know! It's no use your trying to break down a
  stone wall with your head, or exposing your chest to the
  bayonets.

Vera What I simply cannot understand is how the devil did you get mixed up with all those communists!

Ferdinand What? What communists?

Vera Well, ex-comrade Kohout and that lot! What in heaven's name have you got in common with them! You're being very foolish, dear! Why don't you forget about them and go your own way!

Michael We don't mean to suggest it's so easy to break out from this vicious circle, but mind you, it's your only chance, and nobody's going to do it for you! In this respect every one of us is quite alone! Still, I'm sure you're strong enough to bear that solitude.

During the following barrage, Ferdinand gets up and in some embarrassment backs towards the door

Vera Well, look at us! I mean, you could be just as happy as we are!

Michael No reason you couldn't have a place with a face, same as us—

Vera Nice things, pleasant family life—

Michael Neat and elegant wife—

Vera Bright child—

Michael A more appropriate job—

Vera Earn some money—

Michael You could even take a trip to the States, in time—

Vera Eat decent meals—

Michael Dress better—

Vera Go to the sauna—

Michael Invite a few friends home now and then—

Vera Show them your flat—

Michael Your child—

Vera Play them some records—

Michael Bake them some groombles—

Vera In short, the two of you could finally begin to live like human beings!

Michael and Vera, noticing Ferdinand, jump up, astounded

Michael Ferdinand.

Ferdinand Mmnn—

Michael What the hell are you doing?

Ferdinand I'm sorry, I've got to—
Michael Now wait a minute! What's this all about?
Vera Good heavens! Ferdinand!
Michael What's the matter with you?
Vera Come on!
Michael What the hell are you doing standing at the door?
Vera Are you going somewhere?
Ferdinand I'm sorry, I've got to go now—
Michael But where?
Ferdinand Home—
Vera Home? What do you mean, home? What for?
Ferdinand It's late—we've got to get up early—
Michael But you can't do that!
Ferdinand Really, I must go—
Vera I don't know what you mean! This is supposed to be an occasion! A Private View!
Michael We were going to show you around the flat—
Vera Show you all the new things we've got—
Michael We thought you'd finish the bottle—
Vera Eat up the groombles—
Michael Look in on our little Pete—
Vera Michael was going to tell you all about the States—
Michael Vera was about to light the fire—
Vera Michael was hoping to play you our new records—
Michael We were thinking you'd stay the night—
Vera See the way we make love—
Michael We were planning to let you share the warmth of our family hearth which you lack in your own home—
Vera Provide a bit of distraction for you—
Michael Lift you up for a while from the mess in which you live—
Vera Put you back on your feet—
Michael Suggest new ways for you to sort out your present situation—
Vera Show you the meaning of happiness—
Michael And of love—
Vera Harmonious family life—
Michael Life which makes sense—
Vera It was all kindly meant, you know!
Michael We're fond of you!
Vera You're our best friend!

Michael Good God! You couldn't be so utterly ungrateful!

Vera Surely, we don't deserve it! After all we've done for you!

Michael Why do you think Vera spent the entire afternoon baking those damned groombles? Eh? For whom?

Vera Why do you think Michael lugged that darned bourbon all the way from the States? Eh? For whom?

Michael Who do you think we wanted to play those bloody records for? Why the hell do you think I wasted all that hard currency and carted all that flipping stuff across the flaming ocean?

Vera Why do you think I got all dressed up, washed my hair, put on my make-up and the perfume?

Michael Why do you think we went into all this trouble refurnishing this bloody place? Eh? Who do you think we've done all these things for? Ourselves?

Ferdinand Forgive me, but I've really got to go now—

Vera (*very upset; excitedly*) Ferdinand! Listen to me! Good God! You can't leave us here like this! You can't do that to us! You can't desert us! We wanted to tell you so many things! What do we do here without you? What do we do? For God's sake, can't you understand? Don't go! Stay here! Please stay with us!

Michael You still haven't seen our electric almond peeler!

Ferdinand I'm sorry, I must. Well—cheerio! And thanks for the groombles!

Just as Ferdinand is about to close the door behind him, Vera begins to cry hysterically. Ferdinand hesitates, turns, looks at her

Vera (*in tears, crying*) You're an egoist! Disgusting, unfeeling, inhuman egoist! Ungrateful, stupid, bloody traitor! Traitor! Monster! I hate you!—I hate you! Go away!—Get out! (*She runs over to the vase, takes out the roses and throws them at Ferdinand*) Here, take your bloody roses! Take them!— Take them and get out!

Michael Look, Ferdinand! Look what you've done! Really! You should be ashamed of yourself!

Ferdinand hesitates, then picks up the roses and puts them back in the vase

Ferdinand Well, I—I've put the roses back into the vase—see?

Vera? Well, I—I mean, they're back in the vase—I—I'm back.
Oh, all right, I'm sorry—

*At this Vera and Michael relax and return to their earlier, "party"
tone of voice. They both smile. Short pause*

Vera Good gracious! What are we all standing around for? Why
don't we all sit down?

They all sit down again

Michael What do you say about some more bourbon, old boy?
Ferdinand All right with me—
Vera Darling, how about some music?
Ferdinand Michael brought back a lot of new records from the
States, didn't he?
Michael That's right. I did.
Vera Why don't we play Ferdinand that record we were listening
to when he rang?
Michael Good idea! (*He walks over to the record player*)
Vera You'll love it, dear! It's fabulous!

*The same record as at the beginning of the play starts to blare out
full blast*

CURTAIN

FURNITURE AND PROPERTY LIST

On stage: Turkish yataghan
Baroque confessional
Gothic Madonna
Musical rococo clock
Sideboard. *On it:* tray of groombles with napkins
    and spoons
Coffee table
Chairs
Hi-Fi set
Various other antiques

Off stage: Bunch of roses **(Ferdinand)**
Vase **(Vera)**
Tray of drinks **(Michael)**

LIGHTING PLOT

Property fittings required: nil

Interior. The same throughout

To open: Full general lighting

No cues

EFFECTS PLOT

Cue 1	To open *The latest U.S. pop hit record blares out*	(Page 1)
Cue 2	When ready *Doorbell rings*	(Page 1)
Cue 3	**Vera** turns off the record player *Cut music*	(Page 1)
Cue 4	**Ferdinand**: "A bit later, perhaps?" *Clock plays a period tune*	(Page 6)
Cue 5	**Ferdinand**: "Mmnn—" *Clock stops playing*	(Page 7)
Cue 6	**Ferdinand**: "A bit later, perhaps?" *Clock plays a period tune*	(Page 10)
Cue 7	**Ferdinand**: "Mmnn—" *Clock stops playing*	(Page 10)
Cue 8	**Ferdinand**: "A bit later, perhaps?" *Clock plays a period tune*	(Page 16)
Cue 9	**Ferdinand**: "Mmnn—" *Clock stops playing*	(Page 16)
Cue 10	**Ferdinand**: "I remember—" *Clock plays its tune*	(Page 17)
Cue 11	**Ferdinand**: "I know—" *Clock plays its tune*	(Page 18)
Cue 12	**Ferdinand**: "A bit later, perhaps?" *Clock plays its tune*	(Page 20)
Cue 13	**Vera**: "You'll love it dear! It's fabulous!" *The same record as at the beginning blares out full blast*	(Page 24)

MADE AND PRINTED IN GREAT BRITAIN BY
LATIMER TREND & COMPANY LTD PLYMOUTH

MADE IN ENGLAND

www.ingramcontent.com/pod-product-compliance
Ingram Content Group UK Ltd.
Pitfield, Milton Keynes, MK11 3LW, UK
UKHW021820150726
7214IPUK00017B/235